Decorating
for Christmas™

Designs by Sandra L. Hatch

HOUSE of
WHITE
BIRCHES

PUBLISHERS
SINCE 1947

2

Table of Contents

Decorating for Christmas

Decorating for Christmas

I love to decorate my home for Christmas. Quilted items are an important part of the process. I like to have something I have made mixed in with the other Christmas items I have collected over the years.

Most of the quilted holiday projects in this book are quick and easy. They can be made with purchased fabrics, scraps or precut fabric selections like the Jelly Rolls™ or charm packs that are so popular today.

Heart Tree Skirt, **page 40**

If there has ever been any doubt that projects made with Christmas fabrics are popular, one only has to look at the wonderful collections that the fabric companies make available to us each year. I was excited to use some of the latest holiday collections in these projects. Most of them will fit in any style decor.

Whether you prefer the traditional red/green or burgundy/green combinations or the more contemporary pink/green colors, I hope you will enjoy making these projects as much as I did. Your home and the homes of your family and friends will be warmer and more welcoming by adding some quilted holiday cheer this year.

Meet the Designer

Sandra L. Hatch learned to sew at a young age from her mother, grandmother and her involvement in 4-H clubs. She grew up making clothing for herself and her five younger sisters. She even made a few patchwork quilts of the crazy-patch variety. This early interest in sewing led her to pursue a college degree in education to teach home economics to middle school children, which she did for 12 years.

During those teaching years Sandra and her husband had two children and self-built a home. She also made friends with a group of quilters. Through one of these friends she found a new career in the quilting field.

She was editor of the quarterly magazine *Quilt World Omnibook* for House of White Birches. Over the years, Sandra was editor of many special issues and ultimately *Quilt World, Stitch 'n Sew Quilts* and *Quick & Easy Quilting* magazines.

At present time, Sandra is the editor of *Quilter's World*, a bimonthly publication from the House of White Birches. She is also an editor of other quilting publications from the same company. She is the designer/author of *Vintage Quiltmaking* and co-author with Sue Harvey of *Panel Magic*, both books from the Master Quilter's Series. She also co-authored *Putting on the Glitz*, with Ann Boyce.

Sandra enjoys designing and making quilts. She especially likes making quilted items for the holidays and gifts for her loved ones. She also loves to read, spend time with family, travel to warm climates, sit by the pond at her family's camp, enjoy her grandchildren and keep busy.

House of White Birches, Berne, Indiana 46711   DRGnetwork.com

I Believe Banner

Find a preprinted panel or two to frame and hang on a door or above a mantel.

Project Notes

Use a ¼" seam allowance for all stitching. Sew all seams with right sides together.

If you can't find a preprinted panel of the size needed, adjust the size of the finished project by adding or deleting a few of the E-F units as needed. The E-F units are 2" x 2" finished, so the center plus the B/C borders must be divisible by 2.

If the panel that you have is too small, simply add a border around it to measure 8½" x 22½".

To make a table runner that features a beautiful Christmas floral or print in the center, cut an 8½" x 22½" rectangle of the print to substitute for the preprinted panel.

Project Specifications

Skill Level: Beginner
Banner Size: 16" x 30"

Materials

- Preprint panel or panels 8½" x 22½" for A
- ¼ yard green print
- ¼ yard tan print
- ⅓ yard burgundy print
- ⅓ yard burgundy tonal
- Batting 22" x 36"
- Backing 22" x 36"
- Neutral-color all-purpose thread
- Quilting thread
- Basic sewing tools and supplies

Cutting

1. Cut four 1½" by fabric width strips green print; subcut strips into two each 22½" B strips, 8½" C strips, 26½" G strips and 12½" H strips.

2. Cut four 1½" by fabric width strips tan print; subcut strips into (88) 1½" F squares.

3. Cut three 2½" by fabric width strips burgundy print; subcut strips into (38) 2½" E squares.

4. Cut one 1½" by fabric width strip burgundy print; subcut strip into eight 1½" D squares.

5. Cut three 2¼" by fabric width strips burgundy tonal for binding.

Completing the Top

1. Sew B to opposite sides of A; press seams toward B.

2. Sew a D square to each end of each C strip and H strip; press seams toward C and H. Set aside D-H strips.

3. Sew a C-D strip to the top and bottom of the pieced center; press seams toward C-D strips.

4. Mark a diagonal line from corner to corner on the wrong side of each F square.

5. Place an F square right sides together on one corner of E as shown in Figure 1; stitch on the marked line.

Figure 1

6. Trim seam allowance to ¼" and press F to the right side as shown in Figure 2.

Figure 2

7. Repeat steps 5 and 6 on each corner of E to complete one E-F unit as shown in Figure 3; repeat to make 38 E-F units.

Figure 3

8. Join eight E-F units with four E squares to make a side strip as shown in Figure 4; press seams toward E and in one direction. Repeat to make two side strips.

Figure 4

9. Sew a side strip to opposite long sides of the pieced center; press seams toward B-D strips.

6

10. Join three E-F units with four E squares to make a top strip as shown in Figure 5; press seams toward E squares. Repeat to make the bottom strip.

Figure 5

11. Sew the top and bottom strips to the top and bottom of the pieced center; press seams toward C-D strips.

12. Sew a G strip to opposite long sides and a D-H strip to the top and bottom of the pieced center to complete the pieced top; press seams toward G and D-H strips.

Finishing the Banner

1. Sandwich batting between the completed top and prepared backing piece; pin or baste layers together to hold flat.

2. Quilt as desired by hand or machine; remove pins or basting. Trim batting and backing even with the top.

3. Join the binding strips with right sides together on short ends to make one long strip; press seams open.

4. Press the strip in half with wrong sides together along length.

5. Sew the binding to the right side of the banner edges, mitering corners and overlapping ends.

6. Fold binding to the back side and stitch in place to finish. ❖

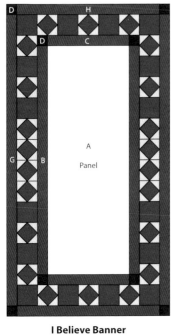

I Believe Banner
Placement Diagram 16" x 30"

Twinkle Star Mantel Cover

Add a country look to your mantel this holiday season
with a pieced-and-appliquéd scrappy mantle cover.

Project Notes

Use a ¼" seam allowance for all stitching. Sew all seams with right sides together.

Project Specifications

Skill Level: Beginner
Mantel Cover Size: 10" on mantle, 9" drop, 60" long

Materials

- 9–2½" x 42" strips coordinating green, cream and burgundy A strips
- ¼ yard gold tonal
- ⅓ yard burgundy stripe
- ⅔ yard burgundy print
- Cotton batting 64" x 16½"
- ½ yard cotton batting
- Backing 60½" x 13½"
- Neutral-color all-purpose thread
- Quilting thread
- Gold machine-embroidery thread
- ½ yard 18"-wide fusible web
- Basic sewing tools and supplies

Cutting

1. Cut each A strip into three varying lengths.

2. Cut two 3½" by fabric width B strips burgundy stripe.

3. Cut two 9⅜" by fabric width strips burgundy print; subcut strips into five 9⅜" squares. Cut each square in half on one diagonal to make 10 C triangles.

4. Cut five 9⅜" x 9⅜" squares batting; cut each square in half on one diagonal to make 10 batting triangles.

5. Trace star pattern given onto the paper side of the fusible web as directed on pattern for number to cut; cut out shapes, leaving a margin around each one.

6. Fuse shapes to the wrong side of the gold tonal; cut out shapes on traced lines. Remove paper backing.

Completing the Mantel Cover

1. Join the A strips on short ends to make five strips at least 62" long; press seams open. Repeat with the B strips to make one long strip; trim to 62" long.

2. Lay the 64" x 16½" batting rectangle on a flat surface.

3. Pin a pieced A strip to the batting matching close to one long edge as shown in Figure 1.

Figure 1

4. Pin a second pieced A strip right sides together with the first pinned strip; stitch along the pinned raw edge through the fabric and batting layers as shown in Figure 2.

Figure 2

5. Press the top strip to the right side and flat onto the batting. *Note: If using polyester batting, do not touch a hot iron on the batting.*

6. Continue adding the five pieced A strips and the B strip until the batting is covered. Trim excess stitched piece to 60½" x 13½".

7. Place two C triangles right sides together; pin a batting triangle to one side. Stitch around the two short sides, leaving the long edge open.

8. Trim batting only close to seam.

9. Turn right side out; press edges flat; machine-baste open edge closed.

10. Topstitch ¼" from stitched edges to complete a C unit.

11. Repeat steps 7–10 to complete five C units.

Finishing the Mantel Cover

1. Pin the quilted C units along the B edge of the quilted base, overlapping corners as necessary to make fit; baste to hold in place as shown in Figure 3.

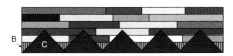

Figure 3

2. Pin the prepared backing piece right sides together with the pinned and stitched top unit; stitch all around, leaving a 6" opening on the long A side; clip corners. Turn right side out through opening; press edges flat and C triangles down.

3. Turn opening edges to the inside ¼"; hand-stitch opening closed.

4. Add more quilting as desired by hand or machine.

5. Arrange and fuse one star shape on each C triangle extending the points into the B strip as shown in Figure 4.

6. Using gold machine-embroidery thread in the top of the machine and matching all-purpose thread in the bobbin, buttonhole stitch around each star shape to finish. ❖

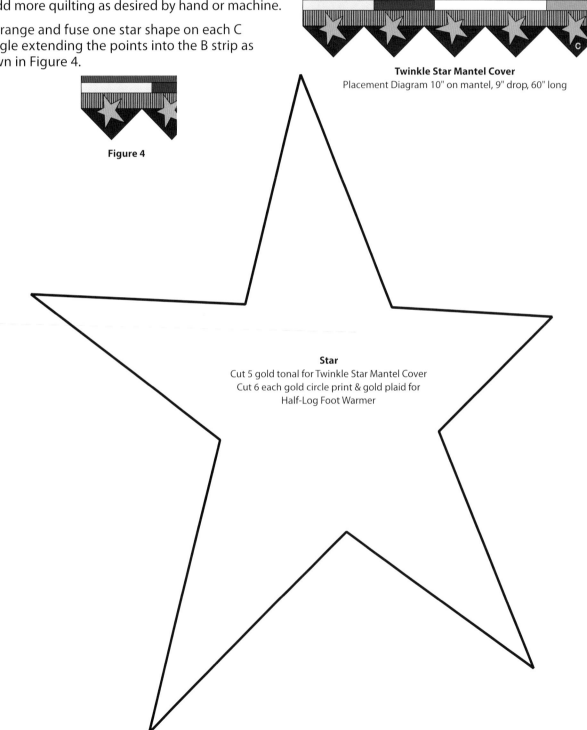

Figure 4

Twinkle Star Mantel Cover
Placement Diagram 10" on mantel, 9" drop, 60" long

Star
Cut 5 gold tonal for Twinkle Star Mantel Cover
Cut 6 each gold circle print & gold plaid for
Half-Log Foot Warmer

Half-Log Foot Warmer

Dress up the bottom of a bed or the back of a couch during the holiday season with a foot-warmer blanket.

Project Notes

Use a ¼" seam allowance for all stitching. Sew all seams with right sides together.

Project Specifications

Skill Level: Beginner
Foot Warmer Size: 84" x 34"
Block Size: 12" x 12"
Number of Blocks 12

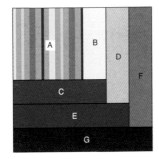

Half-Log
12" x 12" Block
Make 12

Materials

- ¼ yard each gold circle print and gold plaid
- 1 fat quarter each two different gold prints or plaids
- ⅜ yard light green mottled
- ½ yard medium green print
- ½ yard burgundy print
- ½ yard tan print
- ½ yard blue/green/burgundy stripe
- ¾ yard coordinating green plaid
- ¾ yard burgundy circle print
- ⅞ yard burgundy dot
- Batting 90" x 40"
- Backing 90" x 40"
- Neutral-color all-purpose thread
- Quilting thread
- ½ yard 18"-wide fusible web
- Basic sewing tools and supplies

Cutting

1. Cut two 6½" by fabric width strips blue/green/burgundy stripe; subcut strips into (12) 6½" A squares.

2. Cut one 6½" by fabric width strip tan print; subcut strip into (12) 2½" B strips.

3. Cut five 1½" by fabric width J/K strips tan print.

4. Cut one 8½" by fabric width strip burgundy dot; subcut strip into (12) 2½" C strips.

5. Cut six 2¼" by fabric width strips burgundy dot for binding.

6. Cut one 8½" by fabric width strip light green mottled; subcut strip into (12) 2½" D strips.

7. Cut one 10½" by fabric width strip burgundy print; subcut strip into (12) 2½" E strips.

8. Cut one 10½" by fabric width strip medium green print; subcut strip into (12) 2½" F strips.

9. Cut one 12½" by fabric width strip burgundy circle print; subcut strip into (12) 2½" G strips.

10. Cut four 2½" by fabric width strips burgundy circle print. Subcut two strips to make two 26½" H strips. Set aside remaining two strips for I.

11. Cut six 3½" by fabric width L/M strips coordinating green plaid. Subcut two strips to make two 34½" M strips. Set aside remaining four strips for L.

12. Trace star pattern (page 8) 12 times on the paper side of the fusible web; cut out shapes leaving a margin around each one.

13. Fuse six shapes to the wrong side of the gold circle print and six to the gold plaid; cut out shapes on traced lines. Remove paper backing.

Completing the Blocks

1. To complete one Half-Log block, sew B to the right side edge of A as shown in Figure 1; press seam toward B.

Figure 1

2. Add C to the adjacent bottom edge of A, again referring to Figure 1; press seam toward C.

3. Continue adding pieces to the side and bottom of A in alphabetical order referring to the block drawing to complete the block; press seams toward strips after stitching.

4. Repeat steps 1–3 to complete 12 Half-Log blocks.

Completing the Top

1. Join six Half-Log blocks to make a row referring to the Placement Diagram for positioning of blocks; repeat to make two rows. Press seams in one row in one direction and in the opposite direction in the second row.

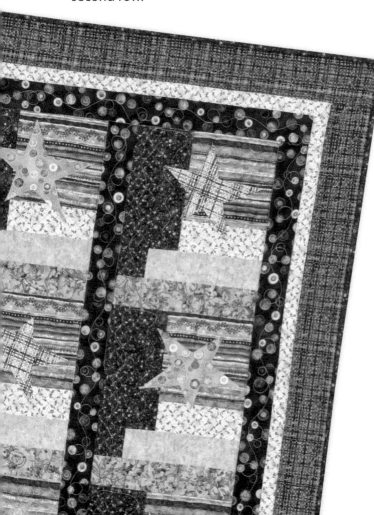

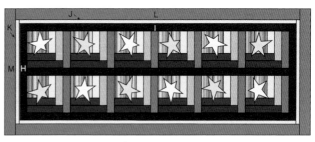

Half-Log Foot Warmer
Placement Diagram 84" x 34"

2. Join the I strips on short ends with right sides together; press seam open. Trim strip to 72½".

3. Sew the I strip to the top edge of the pieced center; press seam toward I strip.

4. Sew the H strips to opposite short ends of the pieced center; press seams toward H strips.

5. Join the J/K strips with right sides together on short ends to make one long strip; press seams open. Subcut strip into two 76½" J strips and two 28½" K strips.

6. Sew J strips to opposite long sides and K strips to the short ends of the pieced center; press seams toward J and K strips.

7. Join the L strips with right sides together on short ends to make one long strip; subcut strip into two 78½" L strips.

8. Sew an L strip to opposite long sides and an M strips to the short ends of the pieced center; press seams toward L and M strips.

9. Arrange a star shape on each block as desired; when satisfied with placement, fuse shapes in place.

10. Shapes may be stitched in place using a straight or buttonhole stitch or left to be stitched in place with the quilting.

Finishing the Quilt

1. Sandwich batting between the completed top and prepared backing piece; pin or baste layers together to hold flat.

2. Quilt as desired by hand or machine; remove pins or basting. Trim batting and backing even with the top.

3. Join the binding strips with right sides together on short ends to make one long strip; press seams open.

4. Press the strip in half with wrong sides together along length.

5. Sew the binding to the right side of the warmer edges, mitering corners and overlapping ends.

6. Fold binding to the back side and stitch in place to finish. ❖

Flying Four-Patch Topper

Make this quick-to-stitch topper to liven up
your table and be ready for Santa's visit.

Project Notes
Use a ¼" seam allowance for all stitching. Sew all
seams with right sides together.

Project Specifications
Skill Level: Beginner
Topper Size: 36" x 36"
Block Size: 12" x 12" and 6" x 6"
Number of Blocks: 5 and 4

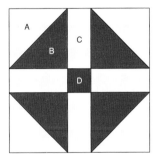

Churn Dash
12" x 12" Block
Make 5

Four-Patch
6" x 6" Block
Make 4

Materials
• 1 fat quarter green print
• ½ yard red plaid
• ⅝ yard red print
• 1⅛ yards cream tonal
• Batting 42" x 42"
• Backing 42" x 42"
• Neutral-color all-purpose thread
• Quilting thread
• Basic sewing tools and supplies

Cutting
1. Cut two 5⅞" by fabric width strips cream tonal;
subcut strips into (10) 5⅞" squares. Cut each square
in half on one diagonal to make 20 A triangles.

2. Cut one 5½" by fabric width C strip cream tonal;
cut the strip in half to make two 21" lengths.

3. Cut one 5½" by fabric width strip cream tonal;
subcut strip into (10) 2½" C rectangles.

4. Cut one 9¾" by fabric width strip cream tonal;
subcut strip into two 9¾" squares. Cut each square
on both diagonals to make eight G triangles.

5. Cut one 2½" x 21" D strip red plaid.

6. Cut two 3½" x 21" F strips red plaid.

7. Cut four 2¼" by fabric width strips red plaid
for binding.

8. Cut two 3½" x 21" E strips green print.

9. Cut two 5⅞" by fabric width strips red print;
subcut strips into (10) 5⅞" squares. Cut each square
in half on one diagonal to make 20 B triangles.

Completing the Churn Dash Blocks
1. Sew the 21" D strip between two 21" C strips with
right sides together along the length to make a
C-D-C strip set; press seams toward C.

2. Subcut the C-D-C strip set into five 2½" C-D-C units as shown in Figure 1.

Figure 1

3. To complete one Churn Dash block, sew A to B along the diagonal to make an A-B unit as shown in Figure 2; press seam toward B. Repeat to make four A-B units.

Figure 2

4. Join two A-B units with a C rectangle to make a row as shown in Figure 3; press seams toward C. Repeat to make two rows.

Figure 3

5. Join the two rows with a C-D-C unit referring to the block drawing to complete one Churn Dash block; press seams toward the C-D-C unit.

6. Repeat steps 3–5 to complete five Churn Dash blocks.

Completing the Four-Patch Blocks

1. Sew an E strip to an F strip with right sides together along length; press seams toward E strips. Repeat to make two strip sets.

2. Subcut the E-F strip sets into eight 3½" E-F units as shown in Figure 4.

Figure 4

3. Join two E-F units referring to the block drawing to complete one Four-Patch block; press seam in one direction.

4. Repeat step 3 to complete four Four-Patch blocks.

Completing the Top

1. Sew a G triangle to two adjacent sides of each Four-Patch block to make a side unit as shown in Figure 5; press seams toward G. Repeat to make four side units.

Figure 5

2. Sew a side unit to opposite sides of one Churn Dash block to make the top row as shown in Figure 6; press seams toward side units. Repeat to make the bottom row.

Figure 6

3. Join three Churn Dash blocks to make the center row; press seams toward the center block.

4. Sew the top and bottom rows to the center row referring to the Placement Diagram for positioning to complete the pieced top; press seams in one direction.

Finishing the Topper

1. Sandwich batting between the completed top and prepared backing piece; pin or baste layers together to hold flat.

2. Quilt as desired by hand or machine; remove pins or basting. Trim batting and backing even with the top.

3. Join the binding strips with right sides together on short ends to make one long strip; press seams open.

4. Press the strip in half with wrong sides together along length.

5. Sew the binding to the right side of the topper edges, mitering corners and overlapping ends.

6. Fold binding to the back side and stitch in place to finish. ❖

Flying Four-Patch Topper
Placement Diagram 36" x 36"

Jelly Roll™ Hexagon Tree Skirt

Strip-pieced triangles create the hexagon shapes that make up the body of this country-look tree skirt.

Project Note
Use a ¼" seam allowance for all stitching. Sew all seams with right sides together.

Project Specifications
Skill Level: Intermediate
Tree Skirt Size: Approximately 40" x 41¼"

Materials
- 2–2½" x 42" strips each light (B and D) and dark (C and E) holiday prints
- ⅝ yard dark green print
- ⅞ yard cream print
- Batting 46" x 47"
- Backing 46" x 47"
- Neutral-color all-purpose thread
- Quilting thread
- 3 wooden buttons
- Basic sewing tools and supplies

Cutting
1. Prepare template for A using pattern given; cut as directed from cream print.

2. Cut one 1½" x 16" strip dark green print for button loops.

3. Cut 264" total 1¼"-wide bias strips dark green print for binding.

Completing the Top
1. Sew an E strip to a D strip to a C strip to a B strip with right sides together along length; press seams in one direction. Repeat to make two B-C-D-E strip sets.

2. Place template A on the strip, aligning bottom edge and cut as shown in Figure 1; turn the template with bottom edge on the opposite edge of the strip and cut referring to Figure 2. **Note:** *Half the units will have light B tips and the remaining half will have dark E tips.* Repeat cutting to make nine each dark- and light-tipped units.

Figure 1   **Figure 2**

3. Arrange and join the stitched units in rows with cream print A pieces referring to Figure 3; press seams toward A.

Figure 3

4. Join the rows to complete the pieced top.

Finishing the Tree Skirt
1. Sandwich batting between the completed top and prepared backing piece; pin or baste layers together to hold flat.

2. Quilt as desired by hand or machine; remove pins or basting. Trim batting and backing even with the top. **Note:** *Avoid quilting too close to one seam from the center to the outside because it will be opened up after quilting for ties.*

3. Using a small plate or a 6" circle, trace and cut out the center of the quilted tree skirt.

4. Cut open one seam from the center to the outside edge referring to the Placement Diagram for positioning.

5. Fold the long edges of the 1½" button-loop strip to the wrong side ¼" and press to hold as shown

in Figure 4. Fold the strip in half along length with wrong sides together and pressed edges even; stitch along the long open edge, again referring to Figure 4.

Figure 4

6. Cut three 4½" lengths from the loop strip.

7. Fold one loop strip in half to make a loop and pin ¾" down from the top edge on one open side of the right side of the tree skirt as shown in Figure 5; machine-baste to hold in place. Repeat at the bottom corner and at the center of the same side.

Figure 5

8. Join the binding strips with right sides together on short ends to make one long strip; press seams open.

9. Press ¼" to the wrong side on one long edge of the strip.

10. Sew the binding to the right side of the tree skirt edges, starting at one end of the cut round center, mitering corners and overlapping ends.

11. Fold binding to the back side and hand-stitch in place.

12. Fold button loops out over the binding; stitch in place at edge of binding as shown in Figure 5. Zigzag-stitch edges of loops together close to stitched end, again referring to Figure 6.

Figure 6

13. Position buttons on the opposite open side of the tree skirt opposite loops and hand-stitch in place to finish. ❖

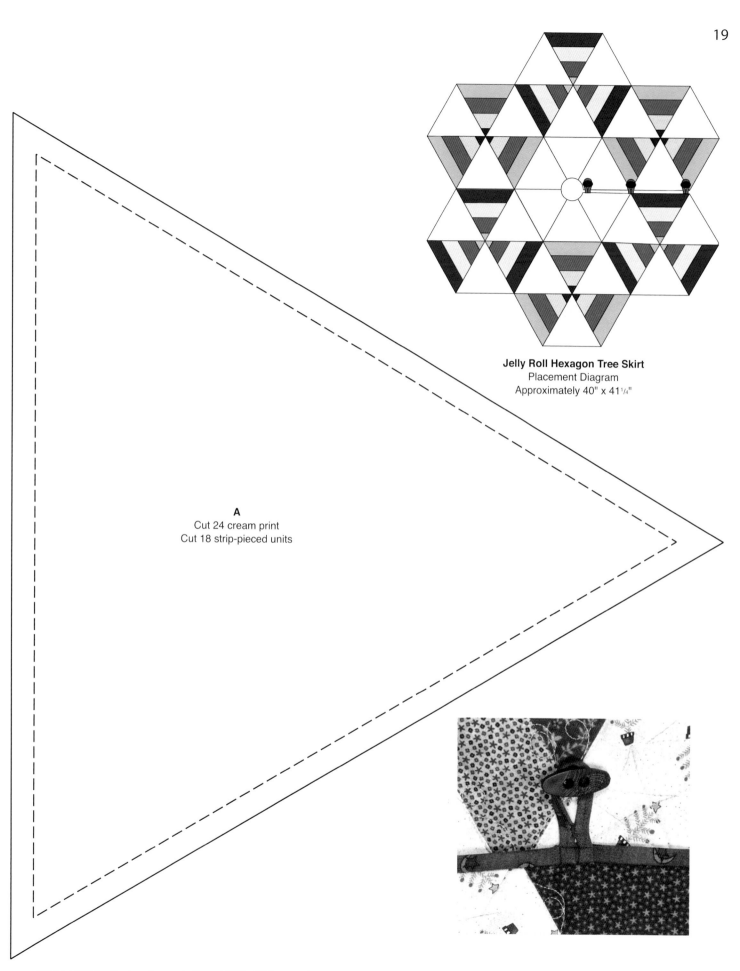

Jelly Roll Hexagon Tree Skirt
Placement Diagram
Approximately 40" x 41¼"

A
Cut 24 cream print
Cut 18 strip-pieced units

Have a Heart Topper

Showcase a beautiful print in the center of this holiday table topper.

Project Notes

Use a ¼" seam allowance for all stitching. Sew all seams with right sides together.

Project Specifications

Skill Level: Beginner
Topper Size: Approximately 43½" x 43½"

Materials

- 1 fat quarter each 8 red prints or tonals
- 1 fat quarter green print
- 1 fat quarter gold-metallic cream print
- ⅜ yard red-with-gold metallic print
- 1 yard holiday floral
- Batting 37" x 37", 2 (10" x 10") squares
- Backing 37" x 37", 2 (10" x 10") squares
- All-purpose thread to match fabrics
- Gold-metallic thread
- 1 yard fusible web
- Basic sewing tools and supplies

Cutting

1. Prepare pattern for heart appliqué using pattern given; cut as directed.

2. Trim the bottom section out of the heart template to the fusible line as shown in Figure 1. Using this template, cut eight pieces fusible web. Remove paper backing.

Figure 1

3. Align edges of fusible web pieces on the wrong side of each heart shape; fuse in place. Remove paper backing. ***Note:*** *Using fusible web only on the edges of the shapes reduces bulk and eliminates any stiffness.*

4. Cut a 31¼" x 31¼" A square holiday floral.

5. Cut (16) 3½" x 3½" B squares total from the eight red prints or tonals.

6. Cut two 3½" x 21" strips green print; subcut into eight 3½" C squares.

7. Cut two 5½" x 21" strips gold-metallic cream print; subcut strips into six 5½" squares. Cut each square on both diagonals to make 24 D triangles.

8. Cut four 2¼" by fabric width strips red-with-gold-metallic print for binding.

Completing the Top

1. Fold the A square vertically and horizontally and crease to mark the centers; place a pin in the crease on each side of the square.

2. Fold four of the heart shapes and crease to mark the centers along the bottom raw edge.

3. Center a heart shape on each side of A using creased lines as guides for placement; fuse shapes in place along top curved edges. Machine-baste raw edges along edge of A together.

4. Sew B to C and add D as shown in Figure 2; press seams toward C and D.

Figure 2

5. Sew two D triangles to B as shown in Figure 3; press seams toward D.

Figure 3

6. Join the B-C-D unit with the B-D unit to complete a corner unit as shown in Figure 4; press seams in one direction.

Figure 4

7. Repeat steps 4–6 to complete eight corner units.

8. Measure and mark 9⅛" from each corner of A as shown in Figure 5. *Note: These measurements might come very close to the edge of the heart shapes.*

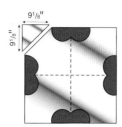

Figure 5

9. Connect marks with a diagonal line, again referring to Figure 5; trim off along the marked line.

10. Arrange and fuse a heart shape on each of the four trimmed corners, overlapping ends over side heart shapes referring to the Placement Diagram.

11. Using gold-metallic thread and a machine blanket stitch, stitch around the curved edges of each fused heart shape.

12. Sew a corner unit to each trimmed corner of A as shown in Figure 6; press seams toward A.

Figure 6

13. Cut each 10" x 10" batting and backing square in half on one diagonal to make four triangles each batting and backing.

14. Place a remaining corner unit right side up on a batting triangle; place a backing triangle right sides together with the corner unit. Stitch around three sides, leaving long edge open as shown in Figure 7.

Figure 7

15. Trim batting close to stitching and backing edges even with corner unit; trim corner. Turn right side out; press flat.

16. Repeat steps 14 and 15 to make four stitched corner units.

17. Topstitch ¼" from the stitched edges of each corner unit; machine-baste open edges closed. Set aside.

Finishing the Topper

1. Sandwich batting between the completed top and prepared backing piece; pin or baste layers together to hold flat.

2. Quilt as desired by hand or machine; remove pins or basting. Trim batting and backing even with the top.

3. Center and pin a quilted corner unit on each side of the quilted top with right sides together with the quilted top, as shown in Figure 8; machine-baste to hold in place.

Figure 8

4. Join the binding strips with right sides together on short ends to make one long strip; press seams open.

5. Press the strip in half with wrong sides together along length.

6. Sew the binding to the right side of the topper edges, mitering corners and overlapping ends.

7. Fold binding to the back side and stitch in place to finish.

8. Fold corner units out flat; press. Topstitch close to seam between the top and the unit to finish. ❖

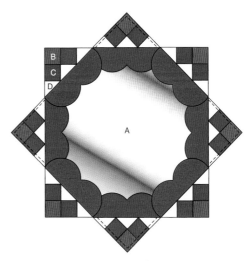

Have a Heart Topper
Placement Diagram Approximately 43¹⁄₂" x 43¹⁄₂"

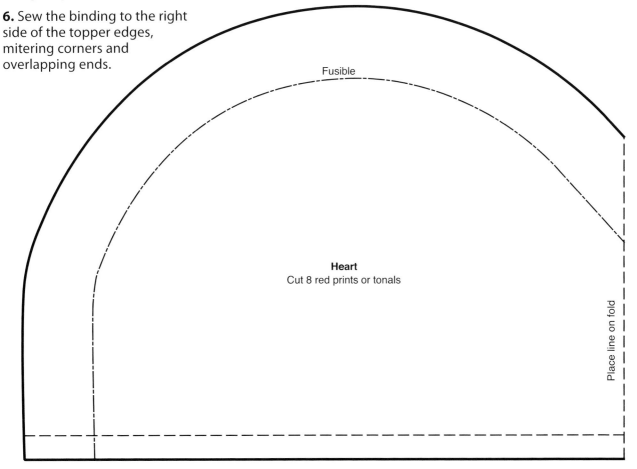

Fusible

Heart
Cut 8 red prints or tonals

Place line on fold

Flower Crazy Stocking

Pretty contemporary colors are used in this lovely Christmas stocking.

Project Notes
Use a ¼" seam allowance for all stitching. Sew all seams with right sides together.

Select a floral print with flowers large enough to cut out separately and stitch to make 3-D flowers.

Project Specifications
Skill Level: Beginner
Stocking Size: 15" x 24"

Materials
- Scraps coordinating prints
- ¼ yard red/green circle print
- ½ yard floral print
- 1½ yards coordinating fabric for backing and lining
- Cotton batting 18" x 27"
- Scraps batting for flowers
- All-purpose thread to match fabrics
- Gold metallic thread
- 7 (½") gold bells
- Paper for pattern
- Basic sewing tools and supplies

Cutting
1. Select seven or eight flower motifs from floral print; cut around shapes leaving ½" all around. ***Note: Do not cut around individual flower petals at this time.*** Cut a same-size backing piece from a coordinating scrap and a same-size batting piece. Pin the batting piece between the flower and backing pieces.

2. Cut two 4" x 10½" cuff pieces red/green circle print; cut a same-size piece of batting.

3. Cut one 3" x 8" loop strip red/green circle print.

4. Set backing/lining fabric aside to cut later after stocking front is complete.

Completing the Flowers
1. Using one layered-and-pinned flower motif and gold metallic thread, straight-stitch around the outside edge of each flower petal to hold layers together.

2. When the petals of one flower motif have been stitched, trim around each petal leaving ⅛" margin from stitching line referring to the close-up photo of one flower.

3. Repeat steps 1 and 2 with all flowers.

Completing the Stocking
1. Using the toe pattern given, and referring to Figure 1, make a paper pattern for the stocking shape. Use a cup or small bowl to create a curved heel as desired.

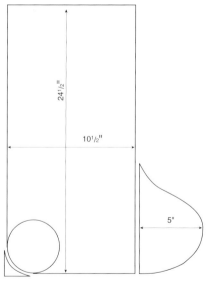

24½"

10½"

5"

Figure 1

2. Using the stocking pattern, cut a piece of batting the same shape.

3. Select a fabric scrap and pin to the center area of the batting stocking piece as shown in Figure 2.

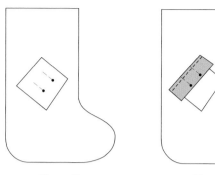

Figure 2　　　　**Figure 3**

4. Select a second scrap longer than the first and place it right sides together with the beginning scrap; stitch along one shared raw edge as shown in Figure 3.

5. Flip the stitched piece to the right side and press flat. *Note: If using polyester batting, do not touch a hot iron on the batting.*

6. Continue to add pieces around the first piece and on subsequent pieces until the entire batting stocking piece is covered.

7. Trim excess even with the edges of the batting stocking shape.

8. Using gold metallic thread in the top of the machine and all-purpose thread in the bobbin, machine topstitch along edges of seams between pieces using a variety of built-in decorative stitches from your sewing machine to complete the stocking front piece.

9. Lay the stocking front right sides together with the backing fabric and cut out one stocking back.

10. Fold the remaining lining/backing fabric with right sides together and cut out two more stocking shapes using the stocking front as a pattern.

11. Arrange the 3-D flowers on the stocking front at least 5" from top edge and ½" from remaining edges; when satisfied with arrangement, pin in place to hold.

12. Stitch 3-D flower shapes in place in the center of the flower; sew a ½" bell in the center of each one.

13. Place the stocking front right sides together with the backing piece; stitch all around, leaving the top edge open.

14. Repeat step 13 with lining pieces except leaving a 4" opening in the bottom of the stocking to use for turning later.

15. Clip curves and turn stitched units right side out; press edges at seams flat.

16. Place the 4" x 10½" cuff piece right side up on the same-size batting piece; place the remaining cuff piece right sides together with the fabric piece. Stitch around three sides, leaving the top 10½" edge open as shown in Figure 4; trim batting close to stitching.

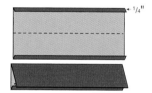

Figure 4

17. Turn right side out; press flat. Topstitch ¼" from edge using gold metallic thread.

18. Pin the cuff to the top edge of the stocking front with backing against stocking and raw edges even; baste to hold in place.

19. To make hanging loop, fold both long raw edges of the 3" x 8" strip under ¼"; fold wrong sides together matching edges as shown in Figure 5; stitch along bottom edge to hold. Topstitch ⅛" from edge on opposite long side.

Figure 5

20. Fold hanging loop and pin to the heel side of the top corner of the stocking front on top of the cuff piece as shown in Figure 6; baste to hold in place.

Figure 6

21. Turn lining wrong side out. Place the stocking shell inside the lining with right sides together; pin to hold. Stitch around top edge.

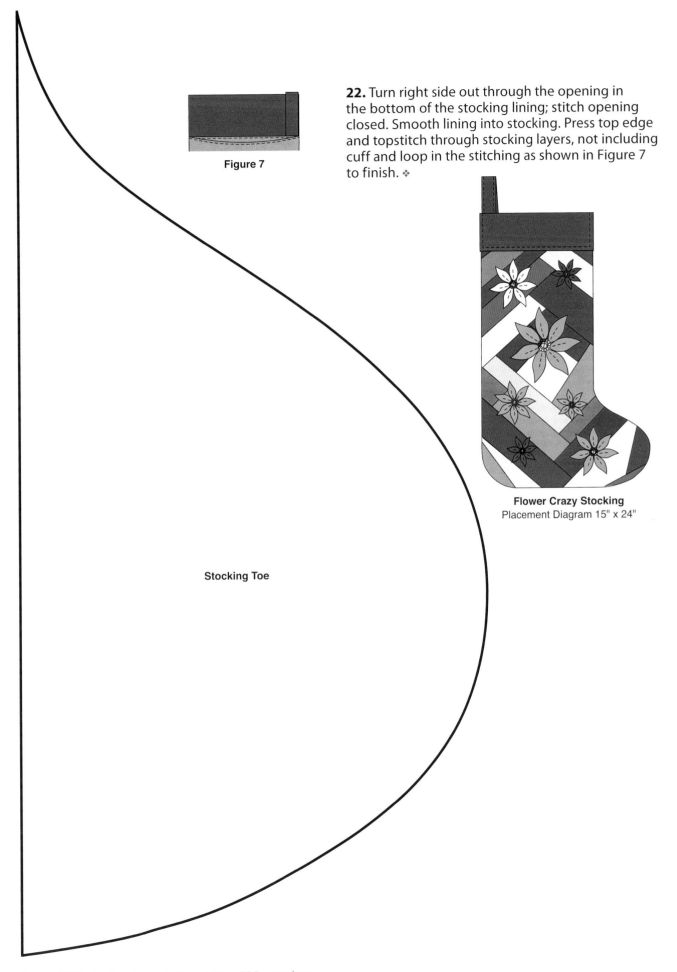

Figure 7

22. Turn right side out through the opening in the bottom of the stocking lining; stitch opening closed. Smooth lining into stocking. Press top edge and topstitch through stocking layers, not including cuff and loop in the stitching as shown in Figure 7 to finish. ❖

Flower Crazy Stocking
Placement Diagram 15" x 24"

Stocking Toe

Stars in the Pathway Runner

Follow the pathway formed by the connecting pieces in this elegant table runner.

Project Notes

Use a ¼" seam allowance for all stitching. Sew all seams with right sides together.

Project Specifications

Skill Level: Beginner
Runner Size: 41¾" x 19"
Block Size: 8" x 8"
Number of Blocks: 6

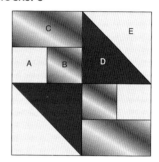

Pathway
8" x 8" Block
Make 6

Materials

- ½ yard green holiday print
- ⅝ yard cream tonal
- ⅝ yard burgundy print
- Batting 48" x 25"
- Backing 48" x 25"
- Neutral-color all-purpose thread
- Quilting thread
- Basic sewing tools and supplies

Cutting

1. Cut one 2½" by fabric width A strip cream tonal.

2. Cut one 4⅞" by fabric width strip cream tonal; subcut strip into six 4⅞" squares. Cut each square in half on one diagonal to make 12 E triangles.

3. Prepare template for H; cut as directed.

4. Cut one 2½" by fabric width B strip green holiday print.

5. Cut one 4½" by fabric width strip green holiday print; subcut strip into (12) 2½" C rectangles.

6. Cut two 2" x 16½" F strips and two 2" x 19½" G strips green holiday print.

7. Cut one 4⅞" by fabric width strip burgundy print; subcut strip into six 4⅞" squares. Cut each square in half on one diagonal to make 12 D triangles.

8. Cut three 2¼" by fabric width strips burgundy print for binding.

Completing the Blocks

1. Sew an A strip to a B strip with right sides together along length; press seam toward B.

2. Subcut the A-B strip into (12) 2½" A-B units as shown in Figure 1.

Figure 1

3. Sew a C rectangle to an A-B unit as shown in Figure 2; press seam toward C. Repeat to make 12 A-B-C units.

Figure 2   **Figure 3**

4. Sew D to E along the diagonal to make a D-E unit as shown in Figure 3; press seam toward D. Repeat to make 12 D-E units.

5. To complete one Pathway block, sew a D-E unit to an A-B-C unit to make a row as shown in Figure 4; press seam toward the D-E unit. Repeat to make two rows.

Figure 4

6. Join the rows referring to the block drawing for positioning; press seam in one direction.

7. Repeat steps 5 and 6 to complete six Pathway blocks.

Completing the Top

1. Arrange and join four Pathway blocks in two rows of two blocks each as shown in Figure 5; press seams in opposite directions.

Figure 5

2. Join the rows to complete the runner center referring to the Placement Diagram for positioning of blocks. Press seam in one direction.

3. Sew an F strip to opposite sides and G strips to the top and bottom of the pieced unit; press seams toward F and G strips.

4. Sew H to two adjacent sides of each remaining Pathway block as shown in Figure 6; press seams toward H.

Figure 6

5. Sew the H/block units to opposite ends of the pieced center unit to complete the pieced top; press seams toward F strips.

Finishing the Runner

1. Sandwich batting between the completed top and prepared backing piece; pin or baste layers together to hold flat.

2. Quilt as desired by hand or machine; remove pins or basting. Trim batting and backing even with the top.

3. Join the binding strips with right sides together on short ends to make one long strip; press seams open.

4. Press the strip in half with wrong sides together along length.

5. Sew the binding to the right side of the runner edges, mitering corners and overlapping ends.

6. Fold binding to the back side and stitch in place to finish. ❖

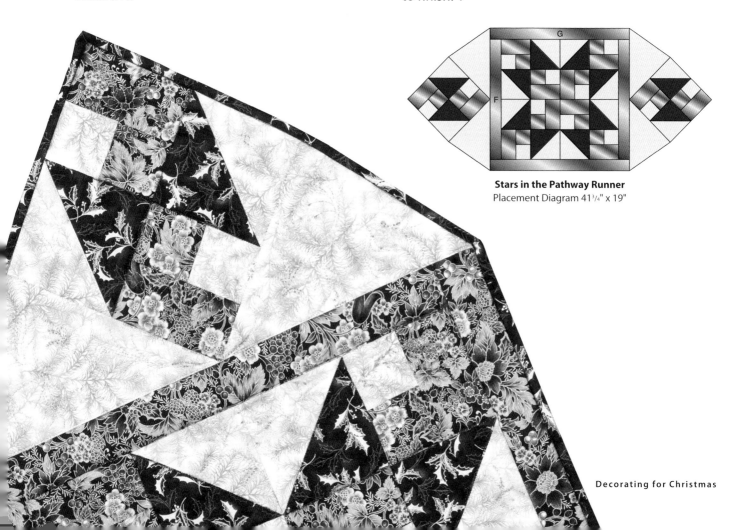

Stars in the Pathway Runner
Placement Diagram 41¾" x 19"

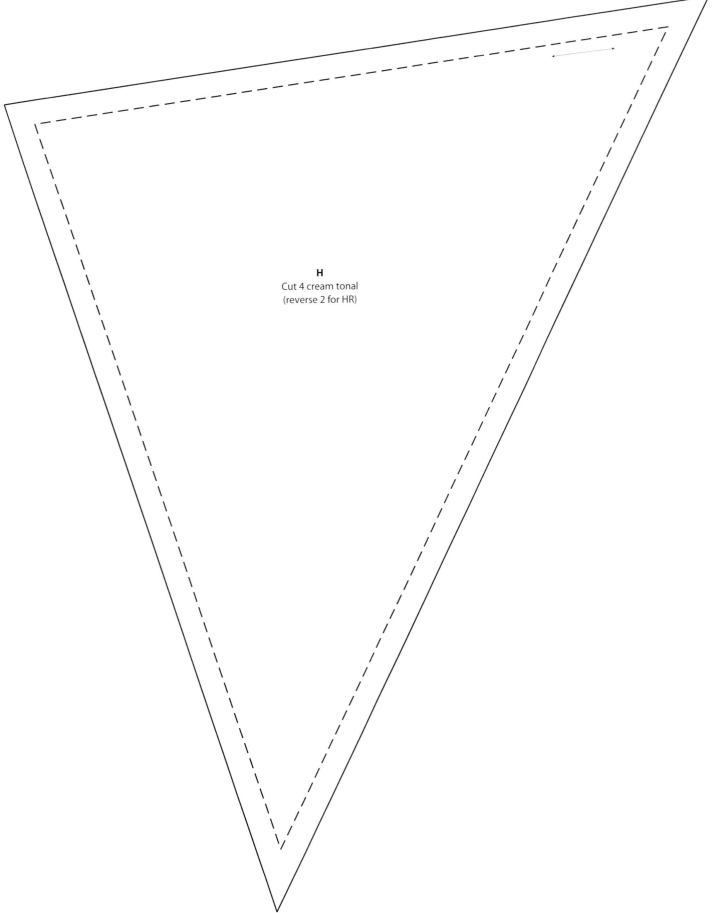

H
Cut 4 cream tonal
(reverse 2 for HR)

House of White Birches, Berne, Indiana 46711   DRGnetwork.com

Yo-yo Gift Bag

Whether you use this as a holiday tote, a shopping bag or a gift bag, you will be in holiday style.

Project Specifications
Skill Level: Beginner
Bag Size: 17" x 19"

Materials
- 10 assorted 5" x 5" scrap squares to coordinate with bag fabrics
- ⅛ yard red metallic print
- ⅛ yard white metallic print
- ⅜ yard black stripe
- ⅝ yard black print
- ⅔ yard lining
- 2 strips batting 1½" x 21"
- Batting 20" x 22"
- Red all-purpose thread
- 10 assorted white buttons
- Basting spray
- Basic sewing supplies and tools

Cutting
1. Cut one 12½" x 34½" A rectangle black print.

2. Cut one 4" by fabric width E handle strip black print.

3. Cut two 1½" x 34½" B strips red metallic.

4. Cut one 3½" x 34½" C strip white metallic.

5. Cut one 2½" x 34½" D strip black stripe.

6. Cut two 7½" x 10½" rectangles black stripe for optional inside pocket.

7. Cut one 19½" x 34½" rectangle lining fabric.

8. Prepare template for circle using pattern given; cut as directed.

Completing the Bag
1. Sew C between two B strips with right sides together along the length; press seams toward B strips.

2. Add A to one B side and D to the other B side to complete the bag top; press seams toward A and D.

3. Lay batting piece on a flat surface; lightly cover batting surface with basting spray. Place the pieced panel on top of the batting; smooth out wrinkles.

4. Machine-quilt in the ditch of all seams and as desired on the A rectangle. *Note: The sample shown was machine-quilted around the ornament shapes in the print fabric.*

5. Machine-baste around all outside edges.

6. Remove the selvage edge from each end of the E handle strip. Cut into two equal-length E strips.

7. Fold one long edge of each E strip ¼" to the wrong side and press.

8. Center a 1½"-wide batting strip on the wrong side of one E strip as shown in Figure 1.

Figure 1

9. Fold the unpressed edge of E over the batting strip and the pressed edge of E on top of the unpressed edge as shown in Figure 2; press.

Figure 2

10. Stitch along folded-over edge along center of each strip as shown in Figure 3. Stitch ¼" from each folded edge of the stitched line as shown in Figure 3.

Figure 3

11. Square up ends of each strip to complete handles.

12. Fold the quilted bag top in half down the length and lay on a flat surface.

34

13. Measure in 3¾" from the edge and pin the right side of one end of one handle to the top right side edge of the bag as shown in Figure 4. Measure in 3½" from the folded edge and pin the opposite end of the same handle right sides together with bag top edge, again referring to Figure 4. *Note: The right side of the handle strip is the side without the overlapped edge.*

3½"   3¾"

Figure 4

14. Turn folded bag top over, align and pin the second handle even with the ends of the handle pinned in step 13 as shown in Figure 5.

Figure 5

15. Machine-stitch over ends of handles several times to secure in place as shown in Figure 6.

Figure 6

16. Place lining piece right sides together with quilted top. Stitch across top edge of bag, stitching over handle ends.

17. Press seam toward lining and topstitch close to seam on lining side as shown in Figure 7.

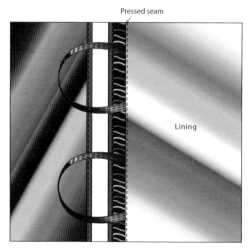

Pressed seam

Lining

Figure 7

18. Fold bag top and lining sections with right sides together as shown in Figure 8. Starting at the bag bottom corner, stitch all around bag top and lining, leaving a 6" opening in the bottom edge of the lining as shown in Figure 9.

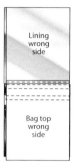

Figure 8   **Figure 9**

19. Trim corners of bag top and lining, and trim batting close to seam at top side seam and along bottom corners to reduce bulk.

20. Turn right side out through opening in lining, making sure corners are completely turned.

Figure 10

21. Press seam inside at lining opening edges and machine-stitch opening closed close to edges as shown in Figure 10.

22. Before inserting lining inside bag, press side seam of bag to help make bag lie flat at sides when complete.

23. Insert lining inside bag. Press lining to the inside at the top edge of the bag. Insert iron inside bag and press lining flat as far inside as the iron will slide. Hold the top side of the bag and insert your hand inside the bag to the corners to be sure lining is completely inside and aligned at corners.

24. Topstitch along top edge of bag ¼"–⅜" from edge.

25. Choose another area on the bag band and machine-quilt to hold lining and bag top layers together to finish bag section.

Adding Yo-yos & Buttons

1. To complete one yo-yo, fold the outside edge of one fabric circle to the wrong side ¼" and hand-baste in place using a double, knotted thread.

2. Pull the thread when you get back to the point where stitching began to gather fabric into a yo-yo as shown in Figure 11; knot thread to secure and cut.

Figure 11

3. Repeat steps 1 and 2 to complete 10 yo-yos.

4. Arrange and stitch yo-yos in place on the C strip, stitching through the center of each yo-yo.

5. Sew a button in the center of each yo-yo.

6. If you want the yo-yos to be more secure, you may stitch the outside edges of each yo-yo to the C strip all around.

Adding Optional Pocket

If you would like a pocket inside your tote, follow the instructions below to prepare lining with pocket before instruction step 16.

1. Place the two pocket rectangles right sides together; stitch all around, leaving a 3" opening on one side.

2. Clip corners; turn right side out through opening.

3. Press opening edges to the inside ¼"; machine-stitch opening closed.

4. Fold the lining piece in half along length; find the center of one folded side. Measure up 3½" from the bottom edge and mark.

5. Center the stitched pocket on one folded side along the 3½" marks; pin and then stitch in place around three sides as shown in Figure 12.

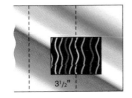

3½"

Figure 12

6. Mark the center of the pocket; stitch a line from the top center to the bottom center to make two sections in the pocket.

7. Complete bag starting at step 16 to finish. ❖

Yo-yo Gift Bag
Placement Diagram 17" x 19"

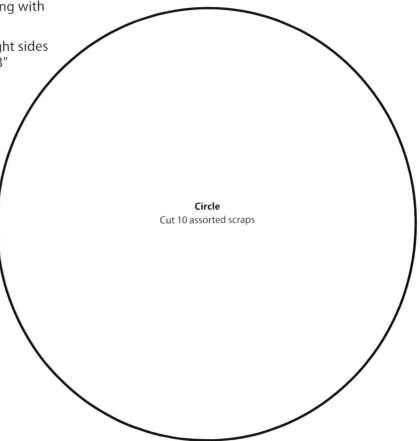

Circle
Cut 10 assorted scraps

Snowball Star

Showcase a beautiful or playful print in the center of the
Snowball Star blocks for a versatile holiday quilt.

Project Notes
Use a ¼" seam allowance for all stitching. Sew all
seams with right sides together.

Project Specifications
Skill Level: Beginner
Quilt Size: 64" x 78"
Block Size: 12" x 12"
Number of Blocks: 12

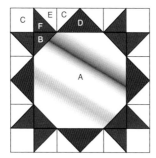

Snowball Star
12" x 12" Block
Make 12

Materials
- ½ yard green tonal
- ¾ yard red/black wavy stripe
- ⅞ yard cream floral
- 1¼ yards cream tonal
- 1⅓ yards red mottled
- 2⅛ yards green floral
- Batting 70" x 84"
- Backing 70" x 84"
- Neutral-color all-purpose thread
- Quilting thread
- Basic sewing tools and supplies

Cutting
1. Cut three 8½" by fabric width strips cream floral;
subcut strips into (12) 8½" A squares.

2. Cut three 4½" by fabric width strips green tonal;
subcut strips into (48) 2½" D rectangles.

3. Cut nine 2½" by fabric width strips cream tonal;
subcut strips into (144) 2½" C squares.

4. Cut four 2⅞" by fabric width strips cream tonal;
subcut strips into (48) 2⅞" squares. Cut each square
in half on one diagonal to make 96 E triangles.

5. Cut five 1½" by fabric width H/I strips cream tonal.

6. Cut five 2½" by fabric width strips red mottled;
subcut strips into (68) 2½" B squares.

7. Cut four 2⅞" by fabric width strips red mottled;
subcut strips into (48) 2⅞" squares. Cut each square
in half on one diagonal to make 96 F triangles.

8. Cut eight 2¼" by fabric width strips red mottled
for binding.

9. Cut six 3½" by fabric width J/K strips red/black
wavy stripe.

10. Cut two 12½" by fabric width strips green floral;
subcut strips into (31) 2½" G strips.

11. Cut seven 6½" by fabric width L/M strips
green floral.

Completing the Blocks
1. Mark a diagonal line from corner to corner on the
wrong side of 48 B squares.

2. Referring to Figure 1, place a B square right sides
together on each corner of an A square; stitch on
the marked lines.

Figure 1

3. Trim seams to ¼" and press B to the right side to
complete an A-B unit as shown in Figure 2; repeat
to make 12 A-B units.

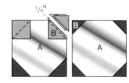

Figure 2

4. Mark a diagonal line from corner to corner on the wrong side of 96 C triangles.

5. Place a C triangle right sides together on one end of D and stitch on the marked line as shown in Figure 3; trim seam to ¼" and press C to the right side, again referring to Figure 3.

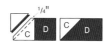

Figure 3

6. Repeat step 2 on the opposite end of D to complete one C-D unit as shown in Figure 4; repeat to make 48 C-D units.

Figure 4

7. Sew E to F along the diagonal to make an E-F unit as shown in Figure 5; press seam toward F. Repeat to make 96 E-F units.

Figure 5

8. Sew an E-F unit to each end of each C-D unit to make a row as shown in Figure 6; press seams toward the E-F units.

Figure 6

9. To complete the blocks, sew a pieced row to opposite sides of an A-B unit as shown in Figure 7; press seams toward the A-B unit. Repeat with all A-B units.

Figure 7

10. Sew a C square to each end of each remaining pieced row as shown in Figure 8; press seams toward C.

Figure 8

11. Sew the pieced C rows to the top and bottom of the previously stitched units as shown in Figure 9 to complete the 12 Snowball Star blocks; press seams toward the center row.

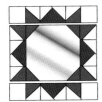

Figure 9

Completing the Top

1. Join three Snowball Star blocks with four G strips to make a block row as shown in Figure 10; press seams toward G strips. Repeat to make four block rows.

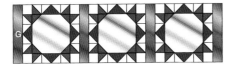

Figure 10

2. Join three G strips with four B squares to make a sashing row as shown in Figure 11; press seams toward G strips. Repeat to make five sashing rows.

Figure 11

3. Join the block rows with the sashing rows beginning and ending with a sashing row to complete the pieced center; press seams toward sashing rows.

4. Join the H/I strips on short ends to make one long strip; press seams open. Subcut strip into two 58½" H strips and two 46½" I strips.

5. Sew an H strip to opposite long sides and I strips to the top and bottom of the pieced center; press seams toward H and I strips.

6. Repeat step 4 with J/K strips to cut two 60½" J and two 52½" K strips. Sew J strips to opposite long sides and K strips to the top and bottom of the pieced center; press seams toward J and K strips.

7. Repeat step 4 with L/M strips to cut two 66½" L strips and two 64½" M strips. Sew L strips to opposite long sides and M strips to the top and bottom of the pieced center; press seams toward L and M strips.

Finishing the Quilt

1. Sandwich batting between the completed top and prepared backing piece; pin or baste layers together to hold flat.

2. Quilt as desired by hand or machine; remove pins or basting. Trim batting and backing even with the top.

3. Join the binding strips with right sides together on short ends to make one long strip; press seams open.

4. Press the strip in half with wrong sides together along length.

5. Sew the binding to the right side of the quilt edges, mitering corners and overlapping ends.

6. Fold binding to the back side and stitch in place to finish. ❖

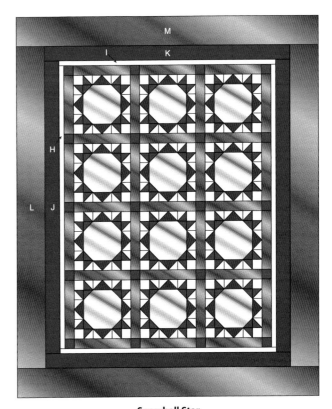

Snowball Star
Placement Diagram 64" x 78"

Heart Tree Skirt

Heart shapes surround the edges of this star-design tree skirt.

Project Notes
Use a ¼" seam allowance for all stitching. Sew all seams with right sides together.

Project Specifications
Skill Level: Intermediate
Tree Skirt Size: Approximately 40" x 40"

Materials
- Scraps green prints
- ¼ yard gold-metallic cream print
- ½ yard each 8 red prints or tonals
- ½ yard red gold-metallic print for binding
- Batting 46" x 46"
- Backing 46" x 46"
- All-purpose thread to match fabrics
- Basic sewing tools and supplies

Cutting
1. Prepare template for heart and A pieces using patterns given; cut as directed. Transfer dots at seam intersections to the wrong side of each A piece.

2. Cut (16) 3½" x 3½" B squares total from the eight red prints or tonals.

3. Cut eight 3½" x 3½" C squares green scraps.

4. Cut one 5½" by fabric width strip gold-metallic cream print; subcut strip into six 5½" squares. Cut each square on both diagonals to make 24 D triangles.

5. Cut two 1¼" x 42" strips red tonal; subcut strips into six 12" strips for ties.

6. Cut 1¼"-wide bias strips red gold-metallic print to total 200" for binding.

Completing the Top
1. Sew B to C and add D as shown in Figure 1; press seams toward C and D.

Figure 1

2. Sew two D triangles to B as shown in Figure 2; press seams toward D.

Figure 2

3. Join the B-C-D unit with the B-D unit to complete a B-C-D unit as shown in Figure 3; press seams in one direction.

Figure 3

4. Repeat steps 1–3 to complete eight B-C-D units.

5. Sew a heart shape to each B-C-D unit to complete a heart unit as shown in Figure 4; press seam toward heart shapes.

Figure 4

6. Join two A pieces, stitching from one marked dot to the other as shown in Figure 5; press seam to one side. Repeat to make four joined units.

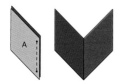

Figure 5

7. Join two of the joined units to complete half the center section; repeat to make two halves. Press seams in one direction.

8. Join the two halves to complete the A pieced center; press seams in one direction.

9. Set a heart unit between each A shape, starting and stopping stitching at marked dots to complete the pieced top; press seams toward A.

42

Finishing the Topper

1. Sandwich batting between the completed top and prepared backing piece; pin or baste layers together to hold flat.

2. Quilt as desired by hand or machine; remove pins or basting. Trim batting and backing even with the top.

3. Using a plate or other 4–6" round object, trace and cut out a circle in the center of the quilted tree skirt as shown in Figure 6. *Note: You may use the circle pattern for the yo-yo given on page 35 to make a circle.*

Figure 6

4. Using a straightedge, cut through one A piece from point to point to make an opening for the tree skirt as shown in Figure 7.

Figure 7

5. Fold ¼" to the wrong side on each long side and on one short end of a tie strip; fold in half to enclose pressed edges to make a ¼"-wide strip. Stitch along open edge to complete one tie; repeat to make six ties.

6. Position a tie at the top and bottom and in the center of each open edge as shown in Figure 8; machine-baste to hold in place.

Figure 8

7. Join the binding strips with right sides together on short ends to make one long strip; press seams open.

8. Press ¼" to the wrong side on one long edge of the binding strip.

9. Sew the binding to the right side of the tree-skirt edges, mitering corners and overlapping ends.

10. Fold binding to the back side and stitch in place to finish. *Note: The binding was folded all the way to the wrong side all around the sample edges except on the open edges and the circle opening; no binding shows on the outside around the curving heart edges.* ❖

Heart Tree Skirt
Placement Diagram Approximately 40" x 40"

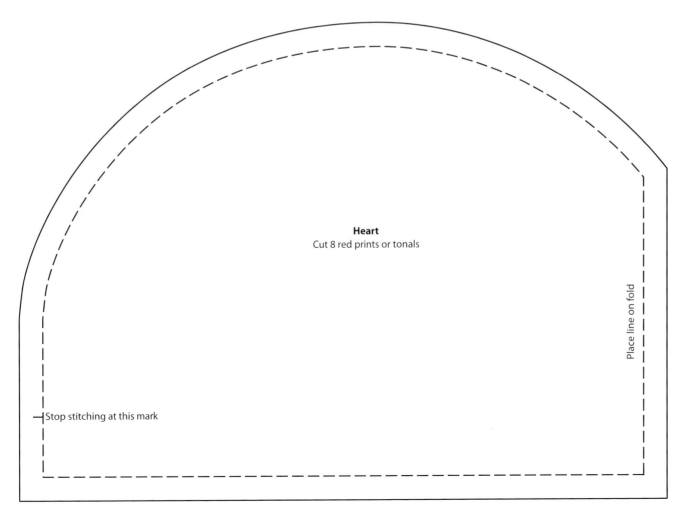

Heart
Cut 8 red prints or tonals

Place line on fold

Stop stitching at this mark

House of White Birches, Berne, Indiana 46711   DRGnetwork.com

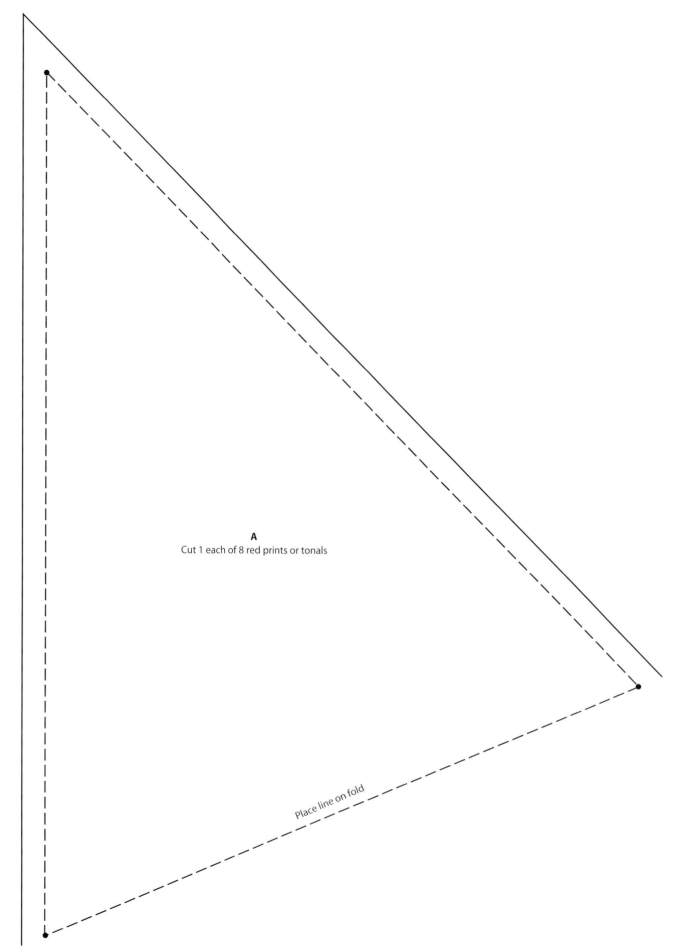

A
Cut 1 each of 8 red prints or tonals

Place line on fold

Cinnamon Sticks Pot Holders

Make a couple of pot holders to match a holiday runner for a coordinated look in your kitchen.

Project Notes
Use a ¼" seam allowance for all stitching. Sew all seams with right sides together.

Project Specifications
Skill Level: Beginner
Pot Holder Size: 9" x 9"
Block Size: 3" x 3"
Number of Blocks: 1 per pot holder

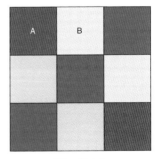

Nine-Patch
3" x 3" Block
Make 2

Materials
- 30 assorted dark green 1½" x 1½" A squares
- 28 assorted light/medium tan 1½" x 1½" B squares
- 1–1" x 42" strip light/medium tan print
- 2–2" x 42" strips cinnamon print
- 2–10" x 10" squares cotton batting
- 2–9½" x 9½" squares backing
- Neutral-color all-purpose thread
- Quilting thread
- 2 (¾") bone rings (optional)
- Basic sewing tools and supplies

Cutting
1. Subcut the 1" x 42" light/medium print strip into four 3½" C strips and four 4½" D strips.

2. Subcut each 2" x 42" cinnamon print strip into two 6½" E strips and two 9½" F strips.

Completing the Blocks
1. Sew a B square between two A squares to make a row as shown in Figure 1; press seams toward A squares. Repeat to make two A-B-A rows.

Figure 1

2. Sew an A square between two B squares to make a row as shown in Figure 2; press seams toward the A square.

Figure 2

3. Sew the B-A-B row between the two A-B-A rows to complete one Nine-Patch block referring to the block drawing; press seams in one direction.

4. Repeat steps 1–3 to complete two Nine-Patch blocks.

House of White Birches, Berne, Indiana 46711 DRGnetwork.com

Completing the Tops

1. Sew a C strip to opposite sides and D strips to the remaining sides of one Nine-Patch block; press seams toward C and D strips.

2. Join two each A and B squares, alternating placement, to make a side strip; repeat to make four side strips. Press seams toward B squares.

3. Sew a side strip to the C sides of the pieced center; press seams toward C.

4. Sew an A square to each end of each remaining side strip; press seam toward B squares.

5. Sew these strips to the D sides of the pieced center; press seams toward D strips.

6. Sew an E strip to opposite sides and F strips to the remaining sides of the pieced center; press seams toward E and F strips to complete one pot holder top.

7. Repeat steps 1 and 2 to complete two pot holder tops.

Finishing the Pot Holders

1. Place one pot holder top right side up on one batting square; quilt as desired by hand or machine.

2. Trim batting edges even with pot holder edges.

3. Place one backing square right sides together with the quilted top; stitch all around, leaving a 3" opening on one side.

4. Clip corners; trim batting close to seam. Turn right side out through opening; press edges flat.

5. Press opening edges to the inside ¼"; hand-stitch opening closed.

6. Add more quilting as desired to hold layers together.

7. Hand-stitch a bone ring to one corner of the backside for hanging, if desired.

8. Repeat steps 1–7 with second pot holder top to finish. ❖

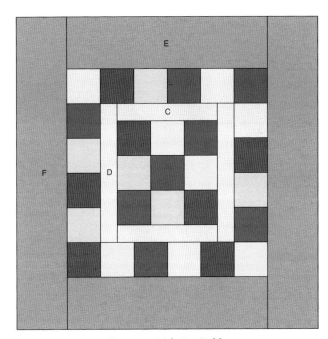

Cinnamon Sticks Pot Holder
Placement Diagram 9" x 9"

Framed Star Candle Mat

Use a contemporary holiday print to make this trendy candle mat.

Project Notes
Use a ¼" seam allowance for all stitching. Sew all seams with right sides together.

Project Specifications
Skill Level: Beginner
Candle Mat Size: 17" x 17"
Block Size: 12" x 12"
Number of Blocks: 1

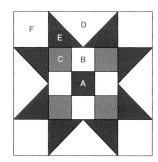

Framed Star
12" x 12" Block
Make 1

Materials
- Fat quarter dark green holiday print
- Fat quarter red holiday print
- Fat quarter holiday message print
- Fat quarter white tonal
- Batting 23" x 23"
- Backing 23" x 23"
- Neutral-color all-purpose thread
- Quilting thread
- Basic sewing tools and supplies

Cutting
1. Cut two 3½" x 21" strips red holiday print; subcut strips into eight 3½" E squares and one 2½" x 2½" A square.

2. Cut four 2¼" x 21" strips red holiday print for binding.

3. Cut one 2½" x 21" strip green holiday print; subcut strip into four 2½" C squares.

4. Cut one 7⅝" x 7⅝" square green holiday print; cut the square on both diagonals to make four G triangles.

5. Cut one 6½" by fabric width strip white tonal; subcut strip into four 3½" D rectangles.

6. Cut one 2½" x 21" strip white tonal; subcut strip into four 2½" B squares.

7. Cut one 3½" x 21" strip white tonal; subcut strip into four 3½" F squares.

8. Cut four 2½" x 21" strips holiday message print; subcut strips into four 8" H strips and four 10" I strips.

Completing the Block
1. Sew A between two B squares to make a B-A-B row; press seams toward A.

2. Sew B between two C squares to make a C-B-C row; press seams toward C. Repeat to make two C-B-C rows.

3. Sew the B-A-B row between the C-B-C rows to complete the center Nine-Patch unit as shown in Figure 1; press seams in one direction.

Figure 1

4. Mark a diagonal line from corner to corner on the wrong side of each E square.

5. Place an E square on one end of D and stitch on the marked line as shown in Figure 2; trim seam allowance to ¼" and press E to the right side, again referring to Figure 2.

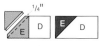

Figure 2

6. Repeat step 5 with E on the remaining end of D to complete one D-E unit as shown in Figure 3.

Figure 3

7. Repeat steps 5 and 6 to complete four D-E units.

8. Sew a D-E unit to opposite sides of the Nine-Patch unit to complete the center row as shown in Figure 4; press seams away from the D-E units.

Figure 4

9. Sew an F square to each end of each remaining D-E unit to make a D-E-F unit as shown in Figure 5; press seams toward F. Repeat to make two D-E-F units.

Figure 5

10. Sew a D-E-F unit to the top and bottom of the center unit to complete the Framed Star block referring to the block drawing; press seams toward the center unit.

Completing the Top

1. Match one straight end of H with the square end of G and stitch as shown in Figure 6; press seam toward G.

Figure 6

2. Repeat step 1 with I on the remaining square side of G and stitch as shown in Figure 7; press seam toward I.

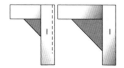

Figure 7

3. Using a straightedge, trim the ends of H and I even with the long edge of G to complete a corner unit as shown in Figure 8.

Figure 8

4. Repeat steps 1–3 to complete four corner units.

5. Stitch one corner unit to each side of the Framed Star block as shown in the Placement Diagram.

Finishing the Candle Mat

1. Sandwich batting between the completed top and prepared backing piece; pin or baste layers together to hold flat.

2. Quilt as desired by hand or machine; remove pins or basting. Trim batting and backing even with the top.

3. Join the binding strips with right sides together on short ends to make one long strip; press seams open.

4. Press the strip in half with wrong sides together along length.

5. Sew the binding to the right side of the candle mat edges, mitering corners and overlapping ends.

6. Fold binding to the back side and stitch in place to finish. ❖

Framed Star Candle Mat
Placement Diagram 17" x 17"

Along the Christmas Trail

If you follow the larger squares you can move
from one corner to the other of the quilt along a trail.

Project Notes
Use a ¼" seam allowance for all stitching. Sew all
seams with right sides together.

Project Specifications
Skill Level: Beginner
Quilt Size: 56" x 64"
Block Size: 8" x 8"
Number of Blocks: 20

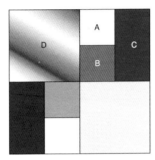

Christmas Trail
8" x 8" Block
Make 20

Materials
- 5–2½" x 42" B strips dark green gold-metallic prints
- 5–2½" x 42" A strips cream gold-metallic prints
- 7–2½" x 42" C strips red gold-metallic prints
- ⅜ yard each three coordinating holiday prints
- ½ yard cream gold-metallic print
- ½ yard green gold-metallic print
- ⅝ yard red gold-metallic print
- 1⅛ yards cream floral
- Batting 62" x 70"
- Backing 62" x 70"
- Neutral-color all-purpose thread
- Quilting thread
- Basic sewing tools and supplies

Cutting
1. Subcut two each A and B strips into 2½" A/B
squares for borders.

2. Subcut five C strips into (40) 4½" C strips and the
remaining strips into 2½" A/B squares for borders.

3. Cut a total of five 4½" by fabric width strips from
the three coordinating holiday prints and cream
floral; subcut strips into a total of (40) 4½" D squares.

4. Cut eight 1½" by fabric width E/F/G/H strips
cream gold-metallic print.

5. Cut five 2½" by fabric width I/J strips green gold-
metallic print.

6. Cut six 6½" by fabric width K/L strips cream floral.

7. Cut six 2¼" by fabric width strips red gold-
metallic print for binding.

Completing the Blocks
1. Sew an A strip to a B strip with right sides
together along length; press seams toward B strip.
Repeat to make three A-B strip sets.

2. Subcut the A-B strip sets into (40) 2½" A-B units
as shown in Figure 1.

Figure 1

3. To complete one Christmas Trail block, sew C to
an A-B unit as shown in Figure 2; press seam toward
C. Repeat to make two A-B-C units.

Figure 2

4. Sew a D square to the A-B edge of each A-B-C
unit as shown in Figure 3; press seams toward D.

Figure 3

5. Join the two pieced units as shown in Figure 4 to
complete one block; press seams in one direction.

Figure 4

House of White Birches, Berne, Indiana 46711   DRGnetwork.com

6. Repeat steps 3–5 to complete 20 Christmas Trail blocks.

Completing the Top

1. Arrange and join four Christmas Trail blocks to make a row as shown in Figure 5; press seams in one direction. Repeat to make five rows.

Figure 5

2. Join the block rows to complete the pieced center referring to the Placement Diagram for positioning of blocks; press seams in one direction.

3. Join the E/F/G/H strips with right sides together on the short ends to make one long strip; press seams open. Subcut strip into two 40½" E strips, two 34½" F strips, two 46½" G strips and two 40½" H strips.

4. Sew an E strip to opposite long sides and F strips to the top and bottom of the pieced center; press seams toward E and F strips.

5. Arrange and join the cream, green and red A/B squares in consecutive color order to make a strip of 21 squares; press seams in one direction. Repeat to make two 21-square strips and two 19-square strips.

6. Sew a 21-square strip to opposite long sides and the 19-square strips to the top and bottom of the pieced center; press seams toward E and F strips.

7. Sew G strips to opposite long sides and H strips to the top and bottom of the pieced center; press seams toward G and H strips.

8. Join the I/J strips on short ends with right sides together along length; press seams open. Subcut strip into two 48½" I strips and two 44½" J strips.

9. Sew the I strips to opposite long sides and J strips to the top and bottom of the pieced center; press seams toward I and J strips.

10. Join the K/L strips on short ends with right sides together along length; press seams open. Subcut strip into two 52½" K strips and two 56½" L strips.

11. Sew the K strips to opposite long sides and L strips to the top and bottom of the pieced center to complete the pieced top; press seams toward K and L strips.

Finishing the Quilt

1. Sandwich batting between the completed top and prepared backing piece; pin or baste layers together to hold flat.

2. Quilt as desired by hand or machine; remove pins or basting. Trim batting and backing even with the top.

3. Join the binding strips with right sides together on short ends to make one long strip; press seams open.

4. Press the strip in half with wrong sides together along length.

5. Sew the binding to the right side of the quilt edges, starting at one end of the cut round center, mitering corners and overlapping ends.

6. Fold binding to the back side and stitch in place to finish. ❖

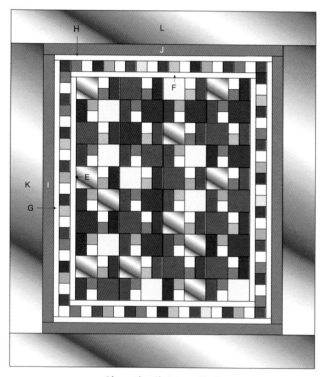

Along the Christmas Trail
Placement Diagram 56" x 64"

Snowball Heaven Runner

Long runners are nice for buffets, pianos or long tables.
Make this blue-and-white snowman runner to last
from the holidays right through the last winter days.

Project Notes

Use a ¼" seam allowance for all stitching. Sew all
seams with right sides together.

Project Specifications

Skill Level: Beginner
Runner Size: 53" x 15"
Block Size: 5" x 5"
Number of Blocks: 15

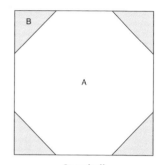

Snowball
5" x 5" Block
Make 15

Materials

- Scraps black and orange solid
- Scrap red mottled
- ⅜ yard medium blue snowflake print
- ⅝ yard light blue snowflake print
- ⅞ yard white tonal
- Batting 59" x 21"
- Backing 59" x 21"
- All-purpose thread to match fabrics
- Black all-purpose or machine-embroidery thread
- Quilting thread
- Black fine-point permanent fabric pen
- 6 black baby snaps
- 6 (⅝") black buttons
- ½ yard 18"-wide fusible web
- Appliqué pressing sheet
- Basic sewing tools and supplies

Cutting

1. Trace appliqué shapes onto the paper side of the
fusible web referring to pattern for number to cut;
cut out shapes leaving a margin around each one.

2. Fuse shapes to the wrong side of fabrics as
directed on pattern for color; cut out shapes on
traced lines. Remove paper backing.

3. Cut two 5½" by fabric width strips white tonal;
subcut strips into (15) 5½" A squares.

4. Cut three 2½" by fabric width strips white tonal;
subcut strips into six 15½" D strips.

5. Cut three 2" by fabric width strips light blue
snowflake print; subcut strips into (60) 2" B squares.

6. Cut four 2½" by fabric width strips light blue snowflake print; subcut strips into eight 15½" C strips.

7. Cut four 2¼" by fabric width strips medium blue
snowflake print for binding.

Completing the Snowball Blocks

1. Draw a diagonal line from corner to corner on the
wrong side of each B square.

2. Place a B square on each corner of A and stitch
on the marked lines as shown in Figure 1.

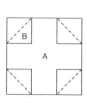

Figure 1　　　**Figure 2**

3. Trim seam allowance to ¼" and press B to the
right side to complete one Snowball block as shown
in Figure 2.

4. Repeat steps 2 and 3 to complete 15 Snowball blocks.

Completing the Top

1. Join three Snowball blocks to make a row; press seams in one direction. Repeat to make five rows.

2. Join the rows with seams in alternating rows going in opposite directions; press seams in one direction.

3. Join three D and four C strips with right sides together along length to make a C-D end unit as shown in Figure 3; press seams toward C. Repeat to make two end units.

Figure 3

4. Sew an end unit to each end of the pieced center; press seams toward end units.

5. Using the appliqué-pressing sheet, assemble the snowman motif in numerical order. Center the assembled motif on one end unit referring to the Placement Diagram for positioning; when satisfied with placement, fuse motif in place.

6. Repeat step 5 to make and position a second snowman motif.

7. Using black all-purpose or machine-embroidery thread and a machine blanket stitch, stitch around each shape except nose.

8. Using the black fine-point permanent fabric pen, outline around the nose.

Finishing the Runner

1. Sandwich batting between the completed top and prepared backing piece; pin or baste layers together to hold flat.

2. Quilt as desired by hand or machine; remove pins or basting. Trim batting and backing even with the top.

3. Join the binding strips with right sides together on short ends to make one long strip; press seams open.

4. Press the strip in half with wrong sides together along length.

5. Sew the binding to the right side of the runner edges, mitering corners and overlapping ends.

6. Fold binding to the back side and stitch in place.

7. Separate the baby snaps; sew two snap halves in place on each snowman for eyes and four to make mouth. Sew three buttons to each snowman front to finish. ❖

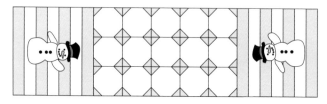

Snowball Heaven
Placement Diagram 53" x 15"

Hat
Cut 2 black solid
⑤

Hat Band
Cut 2 red mottled
⑥

Nose
Cut 2 orange solid
⑦

Head
Cut 2 white tonal
④

①
Right Arm
Cut 2 white tonal

Left Arm
Cut 2 white tonal
②

Body
Cut 2 white tonal

③

Snowman Motif

Twirling Trees Runner

Select holiday-themed fabrics to make a runner for the season.

Project Notes

Use a ¼" seam allowance for all stitching. Sew all seams with right sides together.

Project Specifications

Skill Level: Beginner
Runner Size: 42⅜" x 14⅛"
Block Size: 10" x 10"
Number of Blocks: 3

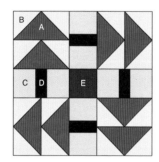

Twirling Trees
10" x 10" Block
Make 3

Materials

- 3–2½" x 2½" E squares burgundy print
- 3–2½" x 42" A strips dark green tonals or prints
- 3–2½" x 42" B strips cream tonals or prints
- 2–2" x 42" C strip cream tonal
- 1–1½" x 42" D strip brown print
- ¾ yard dark green print
- Batting 48" x 20"
- Backing 48" x 20"
- Neutral-color all-purpose thread
- Quilting thread
- Basic sewing tools and supplies

Cutting

1. Subcut the A strips into (24) 4½" A rectangles.

2. Subcut the B strips into (48) 2½" B squares.

3. Cut one 15⅜" x 15⅜" square dark green print; cut the square on both diagonals to make four F triangles.

4. Cut three 2¼" by fabric width strips dark green print for binding.

Completing the Blocks

1. Mark a diagonal line from corner to corner on the wrong side of each B square.

2. Place a B square on one end of A and stitch on the marked line as shown in Figure 1; trim seam to ¼" and press B to the right side.

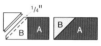

Figure 1

3. Repeat step 2 with a second B square on the remaining end of A to complete an A-B unit as shown in Figure 2.

Figure 2

4. Repeat steps 2 and 3 to complete 24 A-B units.

5. Sew the D strip between the two C strips with right sides together along length; press seams toward D.

6. Subcut the C-D strip set into (12) 2½" C-D units as shown in Figure 3.

Figure 3

7. To complete one Twirling Trees block, join two A-B units to make a tree unit as shown in Figure 4; press seam in one direction. Repeat to make four tree units.

Figure 4

8. Sew a C-D unit between two tree units as shown in Figure 5 to complete a side unit; press seams toward the C-D unit. Repeat to make two side units.

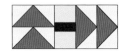

Figure 5

9. Sew E between two C-D units as shown in Figure 6; press seams toward E.

Figure 6

10. Join two side units with the C-D-E unit as shown in Figure 7 to complete one Twirling Trees block; press seams toward the C-D-E unit.

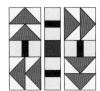

Figure 7

11. Repeat steps 7–10 to complete three Twirling Trees blocks.

Completing the Runner

1. Arrange and join the blocks with the F triangles in diagonal rows as shown in Figure 8; press seams toward F.

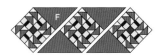

Figure 8

2. Join the rows as arranged to complete the pieced top; press seams in one direction.

Finishing the Topper

1. Sandwich batting between the completed top and prepared backing piece; pin or baste layers together to hold flat.

2. Quilt as desired by hand or machine; remove pins or basting. Trim batting and backing even with the top.

3. Join the binding strips with right sides together on short ends to make one long strip; press seams open.

4. Press the strip in half with wrong sides together along length.

5. Sew the binding to the right side of the runner edges, mitering corners and overlapping ends.

6. Fold binding to the back side and stitch in place to finish. ❖

Twirling Trees Runner
Placement Diagram 42³/₈" x 14¹/₈"

Fabric & Supplies

Page 4, I Believe Banner—
I Believe fabric collection by Nancy Halvorsen for Benartex, Classic Cotton batting from Fairfield Processing and Star Machine Quilting thread from Coats.

Page 7, Twinkle Star Mantel Cover—
I Believe fabric collection by Nancy Halvorson for Benartex, Classic Cotton batting from Fairfield Processing, Star Machine Quilting thread from Coats and 12-weight cotton thread from Sulky.

Page 10, Half-Log Foot Warmer—
I Believe fabric collection by Nancy Halverson for Benartex, Classic Cotton batting from Fairfield Processing and Star Machine Quilting thread from Coats.

Page 13, Flying Four-Patch Topper—
Santa Town fabric collection by Thimbleberries for RJR Fabrics, Classic Cotton batting from Fairfield Processing and Star Machine Quilting thread from Coats.

Page 16, Jelly Roll™ Hexagon Tree Skirt—
Cranberry Wishes Jelly Roll from Moda, Classic Cotton batting from Fairfield Processing and Star Machine Quilting thread from Coats.

Page 20, Have a Heart Topper—
Holiday Flourish 2 fabric collection by Peggy Toole for Robert Kaufman fabrics, Classic Cotton batting from Fairfield Processing, Star Machine Quilting thread from Coats and YLI gold metallic thread.

Page 24, Flower Crazy Stocking—
City Girl Holiday by Kitty Yoshida for Benartex, Classic Cotton batting from Fairfield Processing, Star Machine Quilting thread from Coats and YLI gold metallic thread.

Page 28, Stars in the Pathway Runner—
Holiday Flourish 2 fabric collection by Peggy Toole for Robert Kaufman Fabrics, Classic Cotton batting from Fairfield Processing and Star Machine Quilting thread from Coats.

Page 32, Yo-yo Gift Bag—
Bejeweled fabric collection from P&B Textiles, Classic Cotton batting from Fairfield Processing and Star Machine Quilting thread from Coats.

Page 36, Snowball Star—
Holiday Splendor fabric collection by Yolanda Fundora for Blank Quilting, Classic Cotton batting from Fairfield Processing and Star Machine Quilting thread from Coats.

Page 40, Heart Tree Skirt—
Classic Cotton batting from Fairfield Processing and Star Machine Quilting thread from Coats.

Page 45, Cinnamon Sticks Pot Holders—
Cranberry Wishes Jelly Roll from Moda, Classic Cotton batting from Fairfield Processing and Star Machine Quilting thread from Coats.

Page 48, Framed Star Candle Mat—
Winterscapes fabric collection from Benartex, Classic Cotton batting from Fairfield Processing and Star Machine Quilting thread from Coats.

Page 51, Along the Christmas Trail—
Holiday Flourish 2 fabric collection by Peggy Toole for Robert Kaufman Fabrics, Classic Cotton batting from Fairfield Processing and Star Machine Quilting thread from Coats.

Page 54, Snowball Heaven Runner—
Classic Cotton batting from Fairfield Processing, Star Machine Quilting thread from Coats and 30-weight black thread from Sulky.

Page 58, Twirling Trees Runner—
Cranberry Wishes Jelly Roll from Moda, Classic Cotton batting from Fairfield Processing and Star Machine Quilting Thread from Coats.

All projects professionally machine-quilted by Dianne Hodgkins.

Photo Index

4

7

10

13

16

24

20

28

32

36

48

45

40

51

54

58

Metric Conversion Charts

Metric Conversions

Canada/U.S. Measurement		Multiplied by		Metric Measurement
yards	x	.9144	=	metres (m)
yards	x	91.44	=	centimetres (cm)
inches	x	2.54	=	centimetres (cm)
inches	x	25.40	=	millimetres (mm)
inches	x	.0254	=	metres (m)

Canada/U.S. Measurement		Multiplied by		Metric Measurement
centimetres	x	.3937	=	inches
metres	x	1.0936	=	yards

Standard Equivalents

Canada/U.S. Measurement				Metric Measurement
⅛ inch	=	3.20 mm	=	0.32 cm
¼ inch	=	6.35 mm	=	0.635 cm
⅜ inch	=	9.50 mm	=	0.95 cm
½ inch	=	12.70 mm	=	1.27 cm
⅝ inch	=	15.90 mm	=	1.59 cm
¾ inch	=	19.10 mm	=	1.91 cm
⅞ inch	=	22.20 mm	=	2.22 cm
1 inches	=	25.40 mm	=	2.54 cm
⅛ yard	=	11.43 cm	=	0.11 m
¼ yard	=	22.86 cm	=	0.23 m
⅜ yard	=	34.29 cm	=	0.34 m
½ yard	=	45.72 cm	=	0.46 m
⅝ yard	=	57.15 cm	=	0.57 m
¾ yard	=	68.58 cm	=	0.69 m
⅞ yard	=	80.00 cm	=	0.80 m
1 yard	=	91.44 cm	=	0.91 m
1⅛ yards	=	102.87 cm	=	1.03 m
1¼ yards	=	114.30 cm	=	1.14 m

Canada/U.S. Measurement				Metric Measurement
1⅜ yards	=	125.73 cm	=	1.26 m
1½ yards	=	137.16 cm	=	1.37 m
1⅝ yards	=	148.59 cm	=	1.49 m
1¾ yards	=	160.02 cm	=	1.60 m
1⅞ yards	=	171.44 cm	=	1.71 m
2 yards	=	182.88 cm	=	1.83 m
2⅛ yards	=	194.31 cm	=	1.94 m
2¼ yards	=	205.74 cm	=	2.06 m
2⅜ yards	=	217.17 cm	=	2.17 m
2½ yards	=	228.60 cm	=	2.29 m
2⅝ yards	=	240.03 cm	=	2.40 m
2¾ yards	=	251.46 cm	=	2.51 m
2⅞ yards	=	262.88 cm	=	2.63 m
3 yards	=	274.32 cm	=	2.74 m
3⅛ yards	=	285.75 cm	=	2.86 m
3¼ yards	=	297.18 cm	=	2.97 m
3⅜ yards	=	308.61 cm	=	3.09 m
3½ yards	=	320.04 cm	=	3.20 m
3⅝ yards	=	331.47 cm	=	3.31 m
3¾ yards	=	342.90 cm	=	3.43 m
3⅞ yards	=	354.32 cm	=	3.54 m
4 yards	=	365.76 cm	=	3.66 m
4⅛ yards	=	377.19 cm	=	3.77 m
4¼ yards	=	388.62 cm	=	3.89 m
4⅜ yards	=	400.05 cm	=	4.00 m
4½ yards	=	411.48 cm	=	4.11 m
4⅝ yards	=	422.91 cm	=	4.23 m
4¾ yards	=	434.34 cm	=	4.34 m
4⅞ yards	=	445.76 cm	=	4.46 m
5 yards	=	457.20 cm	=	4.57 m

E-mail: Customer_Service@whitebirches.com

HOUSE of WHITE BIRCHES
PUBLISHERS SINCE 1947

Decorating for Christmas is published by DRG, 306 East Parr Road, Berne, IN 46711, telephone (260) 589-4000. Printed in USA. Copyright © 2009 DRG. All rights reserved. This publication may not be reproduced in part or in whole without written permission from the publisher.

RETAIL STORES: If you would like to carry this pattern book or any other DRG publications, call the Wholesale Department at Annie's Attic to set up a direct account: (903) 636-4303. Also, request a complete listing of publications available from DRG.

Every effort has been made to ensure that the instructions in this pattern book are complete and accurate. We cannot, however, take responsibility for human error, typographical mistakes or variations in individual work.

STAFF

Editors: Jeanne Stauffer, Sandra L. Hatch
Managing Editor: Dianne Schmidt
Technical Artist: Connie Rand
Copy Supervisor: Michelle Beck
Copy Editors: Angie Buckles, Amanda Ladig
Graphic Arts Supervisor: Ronda Bechinski

Graphic Artists: Pam Gregory, Erin Augsburger
Art Director: Brad Snow
Assistant Art Director: Nick Pierce
Photography Supervisor: Tammy Christian
Photography: Matt Owen
Photo Stylist: Tammy Steiner

ISBN: 978-1-59217-263-4

1 2 3 4 5 6 7 8 9